T0131578

# Solving the
# **GRIEF**
## and
# **LOSS PUZZLE**

Other books by Barbara Steingas:

- *Solving the Crohn's & Colitis Puzzle: Piecing Together Your Picture of Optimal Health & Vitality,* pinpoints the top seven body, mind and emotional, and spiritual strategies she used to piece together her picture of optimal health and vitality.

- *The Healing Puzzle: Overcoming A Chronic Illness Through Unconditional Love,* details her own life experiences of being gravely ill and how she put together pieces of a puzzle, along with the love of her late husband, to find recovery.

- *German's Are Funny, Too! Stories of My Cuckoo Kraut Family,* an amusing tale of family life, this book is easy to relate to, regardless of your background.

- *Fluffy The Cat Goes To The Dentist,* is a story and coloring book for children (and the little kid in adults) about how her real life cat had to get a tooth pulled and now has a silly upper lip smile due to the missing tooth.

# Solving the
# **GRIEF**
## and
# **LOSS PUZZLE**
### Piecing Together Your New Normal Life

## Barbara Steingas

Radiant Life Series No. 2

**BALBOA.**
PRESS
A DIVISION OF HAY HOUSE

Balboa Press books may be ordered through booksellers or by contacting:

Balboa Press
A Division of Hay House
1663 Liberty Drive
Bloomington, IN 47403
www.balboapress.com
1 (877) 407-4847

Because of the dynamic nature of the Internet, any web addresses or links contained in this book may have changed since publication and may no longer be valid. The views expressed in this work are solely those of the author and do not necessarily reflect the views of the publisher, and the publisher hereby disclaims any responsibility for them.

The author of this book does not dispense medical advice or prescribe the use of any technique as a form of treatment for physical, emotional, or medical problems without the advice of a physician, either directly or indirectly. The intent of the author is only to offer information of a general nature to help you in your quest for emotional and spiritual well-being. In the event you use any of the information in this book for yourself, which is your constitutional right, the author and the publisher assume no responsibility for your actions.

Any people depicted in stock imagery provided by Getty Images are models, and such images are being used for illustrative purposes only. Certain stock imagery © Getty Images.

Print information available on the last page.

ISBN: 978-1-5043-9892-3 (sc)
ISBN: 978-1-5043-9894-7 (hc)
ISBN: 978-1-5043-9893-0 (e)

Library of Congress Control Number: 2018902566

Balboa Press rev. date: 03/20/2018

Dedicated to my three special men, who
have crossed over to the other side:

George, my late fiancé

Bob, my late husband

Jack, or as I called him, Daddy-O

I refer to them jokingly now as Manny,
Moe, and Jack (a.k.a. the Pep Boys)
whenever they send me a sign in
unison from the other side.

# Contents

"To spare oneself from grief at all cost can be achieved only at the price of total detachment, which excludes the ability to experience happiness.

—Erich Fromm

## About the Author

$B$arbara Steingas is a native of New Jersey and an award-winning, bestselling Amazon author. She is also a Radiant Life Coach and an inspirational speaker, holding a Certified Convention Speaker designation. In addition, Barbara is a member of the National Association of Experts, Writers and Speakers. She has written three other books. The first, *Germans Are Funny, Too! Stories of My Cuckoo Kraut Family*, is a humorous account of her German family. This read spotlights the warmer, fuzzier side of her culture and shows us how we can all learn to laugh at our own family dysfunctions.

Her second book, *The Healing Puzzle: Overcoming A Chronic Illness Through Unconditional Love,* won fourth place and honorable mention in the self-help/inspirational category in a global contest held by a California publishing firm. This book chronicles her inspirational journey of healing from Crohn's colitis, an autoimmune, inflammatory bowel disease, deemed incurable by traditional medicine. And it shows how the power of the unconditional love of her late husband helped heal her. It pieces together the puzzle of her mind, body, and spiritual healing. It has also been developed into a screenplay by Voyage Media Company of Los Angeles, California.

Her third book, an accompaniment to *The Healing Puzzle,* is titled *Solving The Crohn's & Colitis Puzzle: Piecing Together Your Picture Of Optimal Health.* This handbook pinpoints the top seven physical, mental, emotional, and spiritual strategies that she used to regain her health. It offers sample action steps for each strategy and a resource guide at the end of each chapter to help readers find the missing puzzle pieces to their health.

The fourth is a children's story and coloring book titled *Fluffy The Cat Goes To The Dentist.* It tells the tale of how her own cat, Fluffy, knocked her left eyetooth loose and had to get it pulled. Now she has a silly turned upper lip where the tooth was. It's designed to help kids (and adults) who are afraid of the dentist by seeing it through the eyes of a cat.

Barbara is also a physical therapist by trade and has worked for over thirty years at Atlantic Health Systems' Overlook Medical Center in Summit, New Jersey. Using that experience combined with her books, speaking and coaching practice, she is able to help others find their missing healing puzzle pieces and live life radiantly by having optimal physical health, mental and emotional happiness, and spiritual joy.

## Foreword

Having a pathos for grief and loss, I leapt at the chance to write the foreword for Barbara's bereavement book, *Solving the Grief and Loss Puzzle*. When she mentioned this book as I interviewed her for the Central New Jersey newspaper I work for, my arms got goose bumps, which usually happens to me when something really resonates with a higher purpose of its coming into fruition into this world. First, let's go back in time a bit, to when I first met Barbara.

After I spent many days and nights in the hospital with a small bowel obstruction, my aunt showed me *The Healing Puzzle*, Barbara's book about inflammatory bowel disease (IBD). The year was 2013. I just lost my friend, Amy, to Crohn's disease in December 2012 and was on a mission to seek other IBD family members, connect with them, and share their stories, so they would not feel isolated or alone. I created an online support group, ibdjourneys. I wanted to reach out to Barbara since she had Crohn's disease. However, when I met her, Barbara was talking about healing and wellness and other things I was not ready to place in my own puzzle.

Nevertheless, Barbara made it a point to come to visit me whenever I was in the hospital. If she could not get there, she would call. When she did come to see me, being a physical therapist, she would do massage techniques on me, dry sage my hospital room, and print out positive affirmations for me. Soon after, I met a holistic chiropractor and became Barbara's open-minded, but skeptical friend. She invited me to see Dr. Andrew Weil at a speaking engagement, and I still teach my own clients his 4-7-8 breathing technique I learned at this event.

On the day that George, Barbara's fiancé, passed on, I had already grown accustomed to texting her every day, and we touched base many times via phone. On this day, July 31, 2014, I texted her, and Barbara said that George had passed on earlier. I felt as if everything was going in slow motion. I still remember to this day how Barbara asked, "But, Sharon, are you okay? Are you inpatient?" This is when I got to see the incredible resilience that this petite woman has. On that day, I could feel that Barbara was not just trying to grasp at the healing trend; she actually lived it. Was she really asking about my health during a time when clearly she was herself experiencing a traumatic life crisis ... again ... just years after she lost her husband, Bob?

Barbara seemed to be like the Energizer bunny. She takes a licking, and she keeps on ticking, although replace *ticking* with *writing*. Yes, that's right: writing. It became very apparent to me when I interviewed Barbara that writing books became, unknowingly or knowingly, a large piece of her healing puzzle. After her husband's death, she penned and published her first two books. Shortly after George passed on, Barbara completed one book and, just for good measure, wrote two more. When I pointed this out to her during the interview, Barbara just laughed with her infectious giggle and said, "Yes, I guess there is something to that."

Once again, our paths seem to be on the same wavelength. Now that I've finished graduate school and interned with a hospice facility, I am fully certain that the population I will serve will be trauma-based, those with chronic disease, and clients with a terminal illness (hospice). It is my hope to treat this clientele through an integrative and holistic approach encompassing the mind, body, and spirit. When Barbara told me about her grieving puzzle book, I could actually see how it could be pieced together. It is an area of study that we don't talk much about, as death, grief, and bereavement are placed in neat packages in our society and shipped out to funeral parlors and counselors. We are all dying, though. We cannot ignore this impermanence. As a society, we need more books like this in our culture, especially from real stories of those who have been in the trenches and deliver their goods with spirit, who call us out on playing the victim and challenge us to be the heroines and heroes of our own stories. I am up for the challenge. How about you? Thank you, Barbara, for being authentic and for being in my life; I am looking forward to reading many more of your books as you continue your healing journey.

Thoughts and prayers,

Sharon Coyle-Saeed, MSW

CEO/Founder of ibdjourneys

Reiki master, teacher, music therapist, acupressurist, certified crystal healer, integrated energy therapist

Edison, New Jersey

www.sharoncoylesaeed.com

October 2017

## Acknowledgments

I wish to thank all my departed loved ones on the other side, who continue to send their love and support to me. Also, gratitude is bestowed on all the people who helped me through my grieving process. This includes family members still on this side of the realm (especially my mother, Rosemarie, who has been there for me through both losses of the men in my life), friends, coworkers at Overlook Medical Center, bereavement group instructors and fellow participants, Unity School of Christianity (especially their prayer ministry and Daily Word publication), and my mediums: Arlene Petrowsky, Karen T. Hluchan, and Elizabeth Herrington.

In addition, this book could not have been made possible without the help of Jevaux Gall, Mary Ramirez and Joseoh F. of Balboa Press. Special thanks to Sharon Coyle-Saeed for writing the foreword to this book, for her friendship, and for her support, as well. Also, thanks to Stephanie Ward for taking the time to edit this book, despite not feeling well due to musculoskeletal pains. Special thanks also to L. Greg Smith, Wayne Brown, and Chuck Berger, the gentlemen at B.E.S.T. Company, for all their help in marketing my new branding logo and website. The photographer Daniel Torres Jr. did a fabulous job on my photo shoot, and his work in making me look good is well appreciated.

Lastly, I would like to pay a tribute to Louise Hay of Hay House Publishing, who passed away during the writing of this book. Her book, *You Can Heal Your Life*, was the first self-help book I read on my healing journey from Crohn's. I had hoped to fulfill a lifelong dream to thank Louise in person, but instead, I now hope that my words give the ones left behind mourning Louise's passing some comfort. Her light in this world will be missed.

*I still miss those I loved who are no longer with me, but I find I am grateful for having loved them. The gratitude has finally conquered the loss.*

—Rita Mae Brown

## Introduction

Everyone experiences loss at some point in his or her life. Whether it's the passing of a loved one or beloved pet, the breakup of a friendship or romance, a divorce, getting fired, losing a limb, or suffering a natural disaster, it hurts. It doesn't matter if it's a minor or major loss, traumatic and quick or long and drawn out, we all go through a grieving process to overcome it. This helps us to become stronger, to create a new normal life for ourselves.

How we are able to cope with and process our emotions after these losses and tragedies occur will determine how the rest of our lives unfold. We either remain victimized by these experiences, staying stuck in the grief emotions, or we come to some sense of acceptance and explore different ways to experience happiness in our lives.

I first learned about the stages of grief in physical therapy school, when I read *On Death and Dying* by Elisabeth Kübler-Ross. Over the course of my life, I have experienced the usual sad yet expected losses when my grandparents, great-aunts, great-uncles, aunts, and uncles died. However, it wasn't until the passing of my husband, Bob, on April 7, 2008, that I came to know a traumatic loss firsthand. It was through this loss that I had the opportunity to feel what it was like to go through the complete grief process. I experienced all the stages in full depth, including suffering from post-traumatic stress for the first nine months.

After Bob and I had been married for a year, the Olympic skater Sergei Grinkov died on the ice from a heart condition. Being that I felt Bob resembled Sergei, something about that incident shook me up. From that time on, I had an ominous premonition that the day Bob didn't answer the phone or call me back after I called him from work, he, too, would meet his maker. The rational part of me kept saying that I was just being paranoid.

For the next twelve years, Bob answered the phone every time I called, except for two instances, where he didn't for several hours because he didn't have enough signal. During those incidents, I just prayed that he was all right and would call back, and thankfully, he did.

However, on that fateful day in April, when I called him from work, Bob didn't answer or call back. To stay calm as I drove home, I just kept telling myself how he must be out in the yard doing work and to stop being so paranoid. Even when I pulled up in the driveway, got out of the car, and saw our cat Fluffy sitting on the bedroom window shelf that Bob made for her, I calmly said, "Hi, Fluff; where's Daddy?"

As I entered our home, I called out, "Hi, honey. I'm home." No response. I figured he was outside organizing the shed and couldn't hear me, so I went out through the sliding door onto our back deck. Again, no sign of Bob. Then I thought that he must be in the shower downstairs. Being he was six feet and one inch tall, Bob liked the shower stall in that bathroom rather than the tub shower upstairs, closer to our bedroom.

I grabbed the Longaberger basket at the top of the stairs before heading down to put the recycling in the back room. As I got to the bottom of the stairs and closer to the bathroom, I didn't hear the water running or see him standing by the sink, so I knew something was terribly wrong. Like a slow-motion scene out a movie, I dropped the basket to the ground and ran upstairs to our bedroom.

I wasn't prepared for what I saw on the bed, the bed that we had shared since moving into this home in November of 2001. Bob was lying face down, and the television screen was a solid blue, meaning the satellite had turned itself off. Additionally, an empty Gatorade bottle was lying next to him.

With great trepidation, I turned him over and saw his distorted face; he had been in that position for many hours. Bob had suffered a fatal heart attack and was already in rigor mortis. It can't remember how I got the phone in my hand to call 911. I was so distraught that the operator had a difficult time understanding what I was saying, so I had to repeat several times, "My husband is dead!"

His training must have dictated this response: "Do you know CPR?"

As a physical therapist, I took CPR training, so I responded, "Yes." Then I automatically just started performing it, and it wasn't until the third round of the breaths that I realized that Bob's teeth were clenched shut, with part of his tongue stuck in between his teeth, which explained the spot of blood on the comforter. After seeing this, I stopped performing the CPR. Thankfully, the police arrived shortly thereafter to help escort me out of the bedroom into my living room so they could calm me down. Bob was forty-two years old, and it was a month shy of our thirteenth wedding anniversary and a week before we were to go on vacation to Europe to visit my mom and her family.

For the next twelve months or more, I went through an arduous emotional roller coaster of the various stages of grief. Except for the initial shock phase, you never go through it really in succession. The emotions come and go in different sequences; they usually lessen in intensity as time passes over the days, weeks, months, and years following the incident. Slowly, I was able to piece my life back together and found my way back to a happy and fulfilling life, not just existing.

Three years after Bob's passing, I met George at a party for singles. He turned out to be fourteen years older than me, so I was hesitant to keep seeing him, even though we hit it off great and had a lot in common, despite our age difference. I was already widowed once, and Bob had been three years younger than me; he used to jokingly call me his old lady.

On my second or third date with George, just as I was thinking I should stop seeing him before things got more serious, he said something that Bob used to say to me: "What height are you? You're the right height for me." Bob was eleven inches taller than me; he used to rest his chin on my head when he hugged me and say I was the right height for him.

After asking myself, *What did he just say?* I realized that I needed to continue seeing this guy because I knew instantly, my late husband had helped send George to me. After understanding the significance of this important message, I decided that I needed to just be happy in the moment and not worry what may or may not happen in the future. I was hoping that future would be longer, but three years after we met, and just when we were about to be engaged, God took George to the other side on July 31, 2014, via a severe case of diabetic ketoacidosis (high blood sugar level).

This time, instead of finding him deceased, I was in the emergency room of a local hospital with him, holding his hand and looking directly into his eyes, reassuring him he would feel better soon, as the insulin drip had finally arrived. At that moment, his eyes dilated, his upper body and head fell backward (he had been sitting up, out of discomfort) against the stretcher, and he became lifeless. The hospital staff resuscitated him and got him on a ventilator (artificial breathing device) for a couple more hours, but he was basically gone at that moment.

I couldn't believe I was in this situation again. Plus, I had already suffered for so many years; after graduating college, I overcame an incurable autoimmune disease that started in my twenties, and Bob's unconditional love helped me piece together my health. *How much more does God want from me?* I thought. Hadn't I suffered enough in my life already? This was so overwhelming for me to deal with that I went over to the dark side and became like Darth Vader for several days. After deciding to come back into the light, I gradually processed through all the stages of grief, using all I had learned from the past to give me strength and determination to piece my life back together for the third time. Going through the grieving process three years earlier helped me get through it a bit easier. It is truly amazing how resilient we can be when we choose to face our challenges. It makes us become stronger than we ever thought we could be.

This manual contains the physical, mental, emotional, and spiritual strategies I used to get me through the difficult stages of mourning the loss of these two wonderful men I was blessed to have in my life. May this book help you as well get through the struggles and pain of the losses you experience in your life. There's a saying that God (or the universe) doesn't give us more than we can handle, even though we can't always understand this when something tragic happens. It takes time to learn and grow before we can look back and see the changes and the reasons why we needed to go through the challenges in our lives. It's part of our journey to find the true strength and unconditional love within us because without struggles, we could never become all that we were meant to be, to shine our light on the world by giving back those lessons to help others get through their struggles. This is how we transition from being the victims of our story to become heroes and heroines.

Whether you believe in what I'm about to share with you or not, I've come to know through personal experience and with the help of mediums, who are more attuned to the other side, that the spirits of our loved ones are in a loving, beautiful place, and they want nothing more than for us to continue living happy, healthy, and joyous lives because they love us unconditionally, and love never dies. It's what keeps us connected to them and them to us. So on that note, let's travel together through the steps I used to get through the pain and heartbreak. I pray it helps you heal and piece together your new normal life.

### Barbara Steingas

Radiant Life Coach
Physical Therapist
Health and Healing Specialist
Award-Winning Author

barbara@barbarasteingas.com
www.barbarasteingas.com
908.391.4463

"Helping You Find Health, Happiness & Joy"

*Email or call me to schedule a complimentary thirty-minute coaching session.*

*I don't know why they call it heartbreak. It feels like every part of my body is broken too.*

—Chloe Woodward

# CHAPTER 1

♥

## *Body Strategies*

*I*f we don't take care of our bodies' basic needs, we will have a much harder time dealing with tragedy and loss, because our stress factor will increase tenfold or more. It's hard enough finding the stamina to get out of bed in the mornings after a tragic loss, but it's almost impossible if you add on top of that not giving your body the means to have some energy just to get through the day. Also, if you have children to care for, you need to have the energy to attend to their needs as well as your own.

### 1. Hydrate, Hydrate, Hydrate

Crying and stress dehydrate us, so we need to make sure we're drinking enough –specifically, alkalizing beverages like water, herbal teas, and electrolyte-infused water. Herbal teas, such as chamomile, can calm our minds and digestive tracts.

It's easy to turn to alcohol, sugar, and caffeine-based beverages to help us deal with trauma and sadness. Although we all may need that at times, those beverages dehydrate us. Make sure you drink more hydrating beverages, which flush out toxins, to help give you the energy and clarity to deal with your grief.

Furthermore, alcohol may make you feel better temporarily; however, in the long run, it will make you feel worse and cloud your mind and emotions, causing you to stay stuck in the grief cycle. If necessary, go to places like Alcoholics Anonymous for support. There is also Al-Anon for those who have loved ones with alcoholism.

---

**Action A:** Keep a water bottle with you at all times. Stainless steel bottles and filtered water are best. Drink four to eight ounces at least every hour. Set a timer on your phone, if need be.

---

**Action B:** Rehydrate and soothe eyes irritated from crying by placing thin cucumber slices (seedless are best) or tea bags (chamomile or green tea) moistened in lukewarm water over your closed eyes for about twenty to thirty minutes while lying down.

---

## 2. Deep Breathing

When we are stressed or crying, our breath becomes shallow, or we might hold our breath, which deprives us of needed oxygen. That, in turn, will increase our stress levels. Deep breathing helps calm our bodies and minds, and can also prevent or stop hyperventilation. When I am deeply upset or crying, I often hyperventilate, so deep breathing calms me and slows down my breathing. Deep breathing also helps to flush the toxins out of our bodies by moving the lymph fluid (our bodies' garbage-collection system) and prevent us, in turn, from getting sick. When we are stressed, we are more prone to catching colds or other illnesses, and deep breathing can be a preventative technique.

**Action C:** To properly breathe deeply, inhale through your nose as if you're smelling flowers, and expand the lower part of your chest and upper abdominal area as if you're inflating a balloon (you can place your hands there to feel if you're doing it correctly). Then exhale through your nose or mouth with pursed or puckered lips, as if you're blowing through a straw. Your chest will deflate when you breathe out (again, you can feel it with your hands on your lower abdominal area). Try to exhale twice as long as you inhale.

**Action D:** If you are hyperventilating, breathe in and out several times with a paper bag placed over your mouth. Hold the bag close to the opening, and squeeze it with your hand to make the opening of the bag smaller and fit around the opening of your mouth.

**Action E:** Say "Ohm" or sigh while exhaling; this can also be very calming. Also, smelling peppermint, rosemary, or eucalyptus oils can help expand and support deep breathing (see the section on essential oils for proper inhalation technique).

### 3. Proper Sleep, Rest, and Quiet Time

It can be difficult to get to sleep after experiencing a traumatic or a devastating loss. After Bob passed, I had to take an Ambien pill every night for months in order to get to sleep. Finally, I found a natural supplement that helped me fall asleep. Eventually, I healed enough to fall asleep naturally again. I realized after the fact that I had suffered post-traumatic stress in response to both of my men's passing, especially after Bob's death. I could manage to get through the day, but I couldn't unwind enough to fall asleep; it was as if I were on methamphetamines or had ingested a ton of caffeine. The acceptance phase section in the next chapter will tell more about how I was able to get to sleep again naturally.

Symptoms of sleep deprivation, which is one of the worst stressors on our bodies, include decreased immune function, anxiety, irritability, hallucinations, and difficulty concentrating or making decisions. Of course, all these are greatly enhanced with the added stress of being in the grief process.

**Action F:** Find a natural sleep aid. Search on the Web, ask at your local health food store, or consult your doctor for a sleeping aid. Here are some suggestions (again, see the section on essential oils for how to use these):

Roman chamomile: a wonderful central nervous system (CNS) sedative; it's harmonizing, supports emotional stability, and can help you feel centered and safe.

Marjoram: a CNS sedative that supports sleep.

Lavender: a CNS sedative that supports communication of your true needs by helping you speak from your heart.

Sleep diffuser blend: three drops lavender, two drops marjoram, and three drops cedarwood.

---

**Action G:** Try to go to sleep and wake up at the same time each night and morning to maintain a regular sleep-pattern rhythm. Don't eat just before going to bed, and avoid caffeine in the evening. You can also view relaxation meditation videos on YouTube that can help you get to sleep (see the resource guide at end of this chapter for sample links).

---

**Action H:** Take catnaps throughout the day as needed or do a restorative yoga pose by placing your legs up a wall or on some pillows to help get the flow of blood back up into your head.

---

## 4. Eat Properly

Eating can be difficult due to the sadness and possible depression that follows the death of a loved one or a tragic loss. I wasn't able to eat much of anything initially, especially the first twenty-four hours. Because I had gone through the process of healing myself from a chronic, supposedly incurable disease, I already knew the importance of eating healthy and was in the habit of doing so, so I didn't resort to not eating or binge eating. Those eating habits stem from emotional disease and may require professional help to overcome them. But it's okay, in moderation, to eat comfort food that consoles you.

Getting proper nutrition will give you the energy and fuel you'll need to get out of bed and go through the day so you can deal better with all the emotional ups and downs you may feel. Not adding physical fatigue to everything else will make it easier to cope.

---

**Action I:** Eat small amounts regularly and try to eat real natural foods rather than processed foods, quick foods, sugary foods, or fast foods. These can be comforting and easy to resort to but will drain your energy and make it more difficult for you to get out of bed and go through your day.

---

**Action J:** Get your friends and family to cook or provide proper meals for you, as you may not feel physically and emotionally able to cook for yourself. Or if you order food to be delivered, choose healthy foods.

---

## 5. Exercise

Taking walks, especially in nature, or doing other forms of exercise can help to release stress and take our minds off our troubles. Yoga is a great way to relax and unwind to calm our thoughts and ease stress.

Movement is imperative to the flow of the body's blood, oxygen delivery to all the cells and organs, and drainage of lymph fluid. As a result of those processes, it also helps to relieve physical aches and pains. In addition, movement can help prevent depression. Scientists have shown that just by smiling, people felt less depressed, and that's just moving the lips from down to up. In fact, there is a blog by the Huffington Post that is called "The Science of Smiling" by Andrew Merle (huffingtonpost.com/andrew-merle/the-science-of-smiling_b_8570354.html).

---

**Action K:** Make sure to schedule a walk or other exercise at least two to three days per week. I recommend you do it daily during this mourning period. It's best to perform at least twenty to thirty minutes, but any amount is helpful.

---

**Action L:** Gentle stretching (along with deep breaths) is a great way to release stress and emotions. Take a yoga class or other exercise class of your choosing.

---

## 6. Vitamins and Supplements

Stress can deplete the resources inside our bodies, requiring us to replenish needed vitamins and minerals. An extra vitamin B complex and vitamin C tablet, in addition to a multivitamin tablet, is a good idea. During this period of stress and pain, a lot of the reserves of the B vitamins are likely to be depleted in the body, causing us to feel low in energy. To reduce the detrimental effects of toxins produced in the body and to help it fight off illness, I highly recommend vitamin C as a supplement during the grieving process.

In case of an upset to the stomach or digestive tract, ginger, peppermint, or papaya can help. I like ginger and peppermint in herbal-tea form and buy chewable papaya tablets from the health food store. Also, a probiotic can be helpful for the digestive tract, as stress and emotional upset can cause digestive-tract irritation.

---

**Important Disclosure:** If you are taking medications, consult your doctor before taking any supplements or vitamins.

---

**Action M:** Many resources list the vitamins, minerals, and supplements that affect the body during grief. See the resource guide at the end of this chapter for more information.

---

7. **Essential Oils and Herbs**

To restore the body's full capacity and relieve some of the symptoms resulting from the emotional strains in the grieving process, herbal remedies, including essential oils, may also be utilized. These can support you physically, emotionally, and mentally. For example, they can help remove fear, blocks, anxiety, and depression. In addition, they can help with sleep problems like insomnia.

I added this strategy in the physical section because oils are administered on a physical level. It's important to use oils that don't have impurities and are of good quality. They are sold at health food stores or from companies such as dōTERRA and Young Living.

Ways to use the oils:

1. Add six to ten drops to a diffuser.

2. Nasal inhalation: the simplest method is inhaling straight from the bottle. Remove the cap and waft under the nose, inhaling deeply. Ensure that you don't breathe into the bottle.

3. Bath: place five to seven drops in two cups of Epsom salts and place in the bathwater.

**Action N:** Use the essential oils as listed in the other strategies (I placed them with the strategies that match their uses).

Also, there's a nurturing diffuser or inhalation blend for grief itself: four drops bergamot, two drops cypress, one drop marjoram, and three drops of lavender.

Marjoram helps obsessive thinking and releases the pain of your thoughts by easing mental anguish and calming the heart. Bergamot is restorative and relaxing as well as uplifting and helps to release repressed emotions and give you a sense that all will be well.

## Summary Review and Questions

1. Am I drinking enough alkaline fluids? Use cucumber slices or herbal tea bags (chamomile or green tea) to help decrease eye puffiness.

2. Am I taking regular deep breaths?

3. Am I getting enough sleep?

4. Am I getting regular exercise or taking walks?

5. Am I eating good food regularly? Try to eat six small meals per day rather than three larger ones.

6. Am I taking needed supplements like vitamins B and C?

7. Calm your body with essential oils and herbs like lavender.

**Resource Guide: Body Strategies**

lifecellproducts.com/what-are-the-benefits-of-putting-cucumber-on-eyes/

drweil.com/health-wellness/body-mind-spirit/stress-anxiety/breathing-three-exercises/

nutrametrix.com/radiantlife4u

draxe.com/natural-sleep-aids/

lossandfoundxo.com/blog/dont-stress-it-herbs-for-grief-by-the-juice-truck

diynatural.com/herbs-dealing-with-grief/

stillpointstudies.com/essential-oils/blending-grief-essential-oils-heart-chakra

theuntamedalchemist.com/2014/08/27/aromatherapy-for-grief-loss/

aromaticstudies.com/aromatherapy-and-grieving/

herbs2000.com/disorders/grief.htm

youtube.com/results?search_query=meditation+for+grief

youtube.com/results?search_query=relaxation+meditation+for+stress+relief+and +healing

SpiceofLifeYoga.com

usingeossafely.com/inhaling-essential-oils-why-you-should-when-and-how/

Susan G. Niedt, certified clinical aromatherapist/EFT practitioner/consultant/educator, provided information on the essential oils: Susanniedt.goe.ac

The five stages—denial, anger, bargaining, depression, and acceptance—are a part of the framework that makes up our learning to live with the one we lost. They are tools to help us frame and identify what we may be feeling. But they are not stops on some linear timeline in grief.

—Elisabeth Kübler-Ross

# CHAPTER 2

## Mind and Emotional Strategies

As I mentioned in the introduction, I learned the five stages of grief from reading Kübler-Ross's book in college. After Bob passed, I attended a bereavement program that expanded the grief process out to seven stages. I've listed all seven stages here, as I feel it breaks the process down better and describes the full range of emotions you may feel during the grieving process. There are different schools of thought on what the stages are and how many to include. The important thing is that you process through the emotions you feel and eventually come to some form of acceptance of the new normal in your life.

You don't necessarily go through each stage in a linear fashion, in the sense that you feel one until it's completed and runs its course and then go into the next phase. You can feel many of them at once or fluctuate back and forth between them. Also, except for feeling the initial shock, the other emotions listed are not necessarily in the order in which you will first feel them. In addition, you may skip some phases, depending on the intensity of your loss.

## 1. Shock

This is where your whole mind and body go numb. Your life as you know it is gone. Everything is suddenly short-circuited. It's like having your foundation and stability yanked right out from under you, especially if it's unexpected.

I couldn't remember how the phone got in my hand to call 911, and I can't recall giving Bob CPR, even though I knew he had already crossed to the other side, when prompted to do so by the operator. In addition, I became hysterical, and people on the phone couldn't understand what I was saying. The 911 operator had to ask me a few times the nature of my emergency, and my stepmom couldn't understand me, either. My neighbor, who had realized something was wrong and came by, had to take the phone from me and tell my stepmom the tragic news. Also, my knees gave out as I stood in my kitchen and talked to the policeman. He had to brace me from completely collapsing.

When George's eyes dilated and he became unconscious, I became quite distraught and found myself pacing around the emergency ward in a semi-hysterical state. The staff initially tried to send me into the waiting room, but I was too distraught from shock to heed their calling. After several minutes, I had a moment of clarity, probably because I work in a hospital and realized I didn't want to be a disturbance to the other patients and their family members, so I asked the nurse to show us to the waiting room. Thankfully, shortly afterward, a member of the clergy arrived to give us comfort and support.

A little while later, George was taken to the intensive care unit (ICU), and then we were escorted to another waiting room. Not too long after that, I overheard a code being called in the ICU. From work, I knew this meant that someone needed resuscitation. Whenever the doors to the unit opened, I could see them working on a patient in the room directly across from the entrance. I kept asking if it was George, but no one would tell me. All I could do was pace around the waiting room, praying it wasn't him and that he was still stable.

The priest finally came in to update me; the patient in the room I saw had been George, and they were doing all they could to save him. However, their efforts turned out to be in vain, and when the priest came out again, he told me the unfortunate news that George had been pronounced dead. I collapsed in the priest's arms from the shock. He escorted me into the room, and I sat next to George so I could say my goodbyes; one of the nurses wiped a cool washcloth from my forehead over the top of my head, over and over again, to calm me. I never got to see her face or thank her. The rest of the day is a blur to me now, with only small pockets of memory.

The shock phase also puts us in a protective bubble so we can deal with some perfunctory things, like when I had to talk to the police about what happened, plan the funeral, and give the eulogy. Shock provides emotional protection from being overwhelmed all at once. This phase may last for hours or days or a little more.

There is no action step to help you out of the shock phase because by now, you've already experienced it; if you have to experience it again in the future, the initial shock just has to happen and run its course. However, if it goes on too long, then professional help is needed.

## 2. Denial

Shock leads into denial. We can't believe this tragedy is occurring to us. It must all be a bad dream. I felt this fairly immediately while I sat on the couch after the policeman guided me there when our discussion was completed in the kitchen. I remember holding my hands over my ears, rocking back and forth while repeatedly saying, "This can't be happening."

In addition, the first week after Bob passed, almost every morning before waking up, I dreamt that Bob was ringing the doorbell, and when I answered, he said, "Surprise; it was all a joke," meaning he really didn't die. I guess even my subconscious was in denial.

Like the shock stage, denial helps us avoid the pain and keeps us from feeling too overwhelmed. If it's not real, it can't hurt us. So we create a preferable reality to live in until we can gradually accept the full impact of the reality of the event. There's only so much we can handle at one time. However, reality must eventually set in; usually, sooner is better than later, as it will help us transition to the other stages more easily. If it continues too long to be a fantasy, and we deny what has happened, then professional help is needed.

**Action A:** Reach out for support. When you are in denial, it's easy to isolate yourself or to want to save other people from the burden of dealing with your issues. Sometimes, even just sharing your problem with other people can help. Admitting that you don't know what you are doing or what you will do next can help you to feel less out of control by helping to connect you to your feelings. Only then can you begin to find ways to cope with the new reality you are living with.

**Action B:** Writing can be very healing. Write your feelings about what happened. Use a separate journal, or there are journaling pages at the end of each chapter that can be used for this purpose.

### 3. Guilt

Once the protective denial and shock begin to fade, the healing process can begin. At this point, those underlying, suppressed feelings start coming to the surface. One such feeling may be guilt over not doing something different to avoid the situation. We tend to blame ourselves for things like not being more attentive or not seeing the signs. It shows up often as "If I only had done [or said] ..." We should've, could've, and would've all over ourselves.

I blamed myself for not paying attention to my premonitions and for not kissing him good night, not realizing it would be the last chance to ever do so. When Bob came to bed the night before he died, I was already in bed, as he had worked late. A short while afterward, he made this loud snorting sound (it was more than a snore). It startled me awake, and I asked if he was okay. He said, "Yes," and then he fell asleep for rest of night without any further incident. Yet it unnerved me to the point that in the morning, I had to walk around to his side of the bed to make sure he was still breathing before I left for work. I thought if he made it through the night, he should be fine, and I scolded myself for being such a worrywart.

After he passed, I beat myself up a bit, feeling I should have done more. The same thing happened when George passed away. I left it up to the emergency room to do their job and didn't want to get in their way, even though I worked in a hospital for over thirty years. It wasn't until the doctor told me the results of his blood lab, which showed his blood sugar level was over one thousand (it shouldn't get over two hundred normally), that I spoke up, asking the nurse, "Where the hell is the insulin drip?" It had been almost two hours since George had been brought in, and he had only been given one shot of insulin. After he passed, I again beat myself up for a while because I didn't do more, pay more attention to what they were doing, and know more about diabetic ketoacidosis.

What I've come to believe from my experiences is that when our time is up, it's up, and there's nothing we can do to stop it. Otherwise, we will drive ourselves crazy trying to make sense out of something that doesn't make sense. To illustrate my point further, when I was deathly ill and in unbearable pain, I begged God to take me, but it didn't happen, as I was meant to heal from it and go through the grieving process twice in order to help others learn how to heal themselves.

I believe we all have a mission and purpose to fulfill on our journey here; we cross over when it's accomplished or by helping others on the path they need to be on. In other words, we are here for our own growth or to assist others with their growth. So there is nothing we can do when it's someone's time to go, and the sooner we can come to grips with that, the sooner we'll stop feeling guilty and beating ourselves up for not being all-powerful.

That is the job of God (or the universe). All we can do is be the best we can be in any situation at any given time with the skill set we have in that moment.

---

**Action C:** Share your feelings with someone to unburden yourself; it could be a friend, family member, priest, or member of your church. They will help you realize that you're not at fault. There is a destiny of the universe that we can't change. I love the Serenity prayer: "God, grant me the serenity to accept the things I cannot change." Also, "Let go and let God" helps me realize I can't control certain things in life (you can substitute *universe* for *God*, if you prefer).

---

## 4. Anger

It's natural to feel angry over the death of a loved one or a tragic loss in your life. Many times, you either suppress anger because you don't feel it's appropriate or become quite destructive with your feelings of anger. The key is to find a healthy way to release your anger.

After Bob passed away, I was angry at him and God to the point that I cursed them. After finishing my bereavement group program, I found the unread handouts they gave us. I decided it was time to read through them to see if I could get any more value out the program to help me continue my healing process. The page for anger homework was to list who you were angry at. I was no longer in the anger stage, but I wrote down as if I still was, by trying to put down Bob and God, but I accidentally wrote it as Gob. In that moment, I realized it was as if they were joking with me and telling me it was okay to have felt anger at them. It's part of the process.

After George passed away, I became angry almost immediately. I shouted, "Really, God? Are you kidding me? You couldn't let me have George? You're making me go through this again?" Becoming so angry, I not only cursed God, I also became like Darth Vader, going to the dark side by telling God we were enemies. In addition, I said I was done doing this healing work and spreading my positive message. By letting out this anger so intensely, rawly, and honestly, it left my system after only three days. I exhausted it out of me and came to realize that his passing was just part of the journey I signed up for in this life. Then I told God that I was back (like the prodigal son) and that my temper tantrum was over.

It takes time to come to grips with this new normal life you've been forced into. When normal people go through abnormal events, as you can see from my example, they tend to act abnormally. You may feel mad at the person who died or become angry with whoever caused your loss, like a drunk driver, an abusive spouse, or someone who stole from you. People, even family and friends, can do or say the wrong things and make you angry. There may be no particular person you are angry with; sometimes, you just feel mad at the whole world. You may not understand the reason for your loss, and the injustice of it all makes you want to scream in frustration and pain. Maybe you have generalized your anger toward fate, life, or even God for allowing the loss. If you get stuck in anger too long and don't release it in a healthy fashion, then it can turn into rage and bitterness.

**Action D:** Taking deep breaths or exercising can help you release the anger so it doesn't escalate to the point of rage; expressing the anger you feel can help you calm down. It's okay to find a safe place to vent your emotions in the form of yelling, screaming, kicking, or stomping your feet to physically release the anger. Just be sure not to hurt yourself or others; use inanimate objects like a pillow.

**Action E:** Write, draw, paint, or do some other form of art to express your anger. If you write it, then you can rip the paper into pieces and throw them out as a ceremonious way of letting it go and releasing it.

**Action F:** Talk to someone in your support system, or seek professional help. Share what makes you angry; be honest and open with your words, and don't worry about having to sugarcoat it.

## 5. Bargaining

This phase is a desperate round of seeking ways to avoid having the loss that has happened. It's a vain expression of hope to gain some sort of control. You seek to trade something in order to bring the person back (or reverse the situation). It could be trading your life for theirs or saying how you will be totally good from now on if this incident can go away. It can sound something like this: "God, I promise to never do anything bad again if you can bring my loved one back."

I wanted God to take me too and not leave me behind to suffer. In the first week or two, I kept begging God to let me join Bob on the other side. That was the extent of my bargaining phase.

The bargaining process helps us accept the truth of the situation on an emotional and psychological level. It helps us squeeze out a few more moments of our old normal life by clinging to threads of hope before we have to come to terms with the new normal.

**Action G:** Again, the best solution is to talk this out with a counselor (or someone who has been through the grief process) to help you understand that once again, the universe has its destiny, and there are things beyond your control. You can also write down your feelings to help you move through them.

## 6. Depression and Sadness

This is probably the longest phase of the grieving process because you realize the reality of the death or loss. It usually starts out very intense and gradually eases over time, if you allow yourself to move through it. However, the intensity doesn't go down in a linear fashion. It can weave up and down at times, especially when something reminds you of the person or thing you lost.

The first week after Bob passed away, I remember waking up with tears in my eyes. Sometimes, the pain was so intense that I was beyond crying. However, it's important to be able to cry about it to be able to move through this difficult stage. I recently saw the movie *Collateral Beauty*, where one of the characters (played by Will Smith) loses his daughter to brain cancer. He is so distraught, he can't cry or even talk about it. At the end of the movie, his wife helps him cry and talk about what happened by showing him a video of him playing with his daughter when she was still alive and healthy.

I was blessed to have people with me for practically the entire time I grieved. Bob's family was with me for the first week, as we all stayed at my sister-in-law's home. Then I went to Germany for two weeks to be with my mother. Afterward, my best friend stayed with me until Mom arrived for a three-month stay. I also had my furry child, Fluffy the cat, who was always by my side. I don't know if I could have slept in my bed again or continued to stay in my home without her.

The point is, we need to surround ourselves with support. It's okay to have some time alone, and in fact, that's almost as important; we need time to unwind and relax and rest. We need some time alone to feel our feelings and not just keep ourselves distracted to avoid the pain and despair we feel (although we don't want to isolate ourselves too much, as that's a sign of clinical depression).

Another blessing was that I took a three-month paid leave of absence from my job to allow me time to heal. The thought of going to work initially made me nauseous; I'm a physical therapist in a hospital, where I help people to get stronger. I normally love helping my patients, but I didn't know how I could do it with joy and passion in the frame of mind I was in, and I wasn't able to fake it. No patient wants a sad or depressed health care worker. Also, I could break down and cry at any moment, which wouldn't be fair to my patients and coworkers.

Being in crowds, like when I went shopping with my mom, was tough. At times, I would freak out about having too many people close to me or if I was blocked from pushing the cart through an aisle. It's important to take the time you need, if possible. On the other hand, some people prefer to keep working to keep them sane and give them a routine. Do what works best for you to cope.

Thankfully, my employer also provides us with a counseling service; I got up to ten visits free of charge to help me work through all these stages of grief. Seek whatever resources are afforded to you and take advantage of them. There are also free support groups and bereavement programs.

**Action H:** Find support groups, counselors, or a priest or pastor.

**Action I:** Again, journaling is very healing. Essential oils such as wild orange, bergamot, frankincense, and grapefruit are also helpful in lifting depression. A lovely blend for the diffuser for depression is three drops bergamot, two drops basil, one drop geranium, and two drops frankincense.

**Action J:** Seek professional help from counselor, psychologist, or psychiatrist.

## 7. Acceptance

This is the last phase; the goal of going through the grief process is coming to some sort of acceptance of our new normal life. Challenges help us grow and become stronger if we allow it. At some point in our lives, we are all victims of circumstances beyond our control. However, it's part of our hero or heroine journey if we can rise above our challenges and not stay the victim.

Acceptance does not mean we pretend that it has not happened. Acceptance means embracing the present, with both its good and bad, in order to shape our new future. We can still think about our loved ones. Our current life has been touched by them having been in our lives, so it's important to reflect upon those good times and cherish that, without dwelling on that past life too much, or you won't be able to move forward with your new life and bring happiness and joy to your life.

Acceptance can begin by just having more good days than bad ones or by taking responsibility for your actions and accomplishing tasks. In addition, a sign of acceptance is being willing to change your behavior in response to the needs of others. You begin to be more content as you journey toward a more normalized new life.

Our loved ones want us to be happy and continue to live our lives. I feel we honor them by doing just that. Their spirits are happy and fine on the other side (at least, that's what my experience has been). I had post-traumatic stress after both Bob and George passed away; after Bob died, I couldn't fall asleep and needed Ambien. Besides using a natural sleeping aid, what helped me get off Ambien was going to see a medium (a person who is able to communicate with the other side). Both times, I was told so many beautiful things from both Bob and George, which healed me so much that I could fall asleep again without needing the medication.

---

**Action K:** Return to your normal routine. For example, go back to work, get together with friends you haven't seen in a while, do an activity you stopped but enjoy, or learn a new hobby. About a year after Bob died, I finally started writing again. I knew it was something he would've wanted me to do.

**Action L:** The essential oil spikenard helps to calm emotions and encourages acceptance. Cypress oil helps to release the past and to look forward by helping you flow into who you are truly meant to be. Helichrysum oil supports acceptance and calms painful emotions so you can be open to healing and accepting love. This oil is often used for post-traumatic stress disorder (PTSD).

## Summary Review and Questions

1. Allow yourself the time you need to be in the shock stage before having to experience and process the other emotions that will arise.

2. What are you in denial about in the situation? How can you help yourself move out of denial?

3. What are you feeling guilty about that you wish you could've done differently? Realize that in the end, we can't change other people's destiny; things happen in life the way they are supposed to turn out, even if we can't understand or explain it.

4. Who or what are you angry with?

5. What bargains are you making with God (or the universe)?

6. Sadness and short-term depression are normal, especially around the holidays, when it can be tougher. Seek out support groups or a grief counselor; if it becomes long-term and interferes with you getting back to a new normal life, then seek other professional avenues for help. Use journaling to write down your feelings. Do something nice for yourself, like get a massage to help you unwind.

7. Eventually, find acceptance of this new normal life and feel hopeful about the new future that life has in store for you.

## Resource Guide: Emotional and Mental Strategies

*On Death and Dying,* by Elisabeth Kübler-Ross

en.wikipedia.org/wiki/K%C3%BCbler-Ross_model

grief.com/the-five-stages-of-grief/

huffingtonpost.com/megan-devine/stages-of-grief_b_4414077.html

econdolence.com/learn/topic/grief-coping/

helpguide.org/articles/grief/coping-with-grief-and-loss.htm

betterhelp.com/helpme/?utm_source=AdWords&utm_medium=Search_PPC_c&utm_term=processing+grief+and+loss_b&utm_content=27452371690&network=s&placement=&target=&matchtype=b&utm_campaign=384672130&ad_type=text&adposition=1t1&gclid=EAIaIQobChMI9_Piz8P41QIVD5FpCh3doADtEAAYASAAEglvoPD_BwE&gor=helpme

cdcr.ca.gov/Wellness/docs/Grief-Of-Parents-Lifetime-Journey.pdf

complicatedgrief.columbia.edu/resources/resources-public/websites/

newyorker.com/books/page-turner/
a-reading-list-for-the-grieving

*Back to Life: Your Personal Guidebook to Grief Recovery,* by Jennie Wright

# Chapter 3

♥

## *Spiritual Strategies*

On the topic of spiritual strategies, I am not speaking about any religious belief but rather your spirit or soul. Having faith in and a connection with something bigger than yourself and the loss you are experiencing is paramount in being able to move through the grieving process. This could be the universe, God, Jesus, Buddha, or Mohammed to name a few, whatever supreme being or energy that you lean on for comfort and hope.

After Bob died, someone sent a card to my sister-in-law that gave me comfort and helped me to understand what had happened. It said how life is like a needlepoint; we see the underside, which is chaotic, ugly, and seems to have no reason or rhyme to it. That's the side we tend to see, which is why we can't understand tragic circumstances we experience in life. However, when the needlepoint is turned over, it's a beautiful, cohesive picture, where everything falls into place and has total meaning. That's the side God sees. So when we can start to see life from God's (or the universe's) perspective, the events and experiences in our lives begin to make some sense.

Spiritual strategies helped me to move through the emotional phases more quickly. We each have our own beliefs based on religion, even atheists; this chapter is not about any religious doctrine. I'm not trying to convert anyone to my beliefs. The strategies I list in this chapter are ones that helped me. It's my hope to give you a starting point of eclectic ideas. However, I can only teach from what I know and my belief perspective, which does include God.

## 1. Meditation

Meditation is a practice of concentrated focus upon a sound, object, visualization, breath, or movement in order to reduce stress, promote relaxation, and enhance personal and spiritual growth. It can also re-energize and replenish you.

You can sit or lie down to meditate; keep your eyes closed or softly opened, gazing into the distance or at an object. Focus on your breathing or a word repeated over and over or listen to a meditation CD or YouTube video.

You can also perform movement meditation by listening to music while performing free-form movement or dance. This type of meditation is helpful to those who find it difficult to remain still.

Yoga classes also incorporate meditation in some format.

We all benefit from some daily downtime to give our brains a break and escape from our nonstop lives, so we can reflect and listen to our inner voice, not just what the outside world tells us. Therefore, meditation is even more important when we are going through stressful times; it can help us relax and feel some peace, even if only momentarily. Meditation also helps us physically by lowering our blood pressure, improving our immune and digestive systems, calming our emotions, and improving our spiritual connections, thereby allowing us to deal with stressors much more effectively.

**Action A:** Find a form of meditation that works for you. You can search online for a formalized meditation practice, go to a yoga class, watch a sunset, or tend a garden, to name a few ideas. Practice some form of meditation at least once a day for a minimum of five to ten minutes (however, twenty to thirty minutes is more beneficial). The essential oils of sandalwood, frankincense, and juniper berry can help aid in meditation.

## 2. Positive Thoughts

Shifting your focus away from the negativity of the situation can help give you hope. It's a matter of looking at the glass as half-full, rather than half-empty. There's always something positive, no matter how small, in every situation, no matter how bad you may be feeling. Also, humor is a good way to release the tension and stress of loss. The night before Bob's funeral, his family (including me) gathered at his sister's home. We had comic relief from his twin siblings, who talked about their high school antics and how my sister-in-law was into Gumby.

Remember the happy times you spent with this person while they were alive, things they taught you or how they helped you grow. This is bittersweet because sometimes, there's also sadness because they're no longer there, but it may bring you some temporary joy. Over time, the bittersweet tends to fade, and you can feel just happiness for the time you spent with them. This has been my experience, and although the bittersweetness does occasionally pop into my heart, the happiness outweighs it by far.

These brief periods of positive thoughts help break up the grief and give your mind some happiness to remember, so you don't get lost in the complete darkness of depression and despair. I like to read *The Daily Word* by the Unity School of Christianity. It gives a positive affirmation each day. It took me about five months after Bob died before I could feel the benefit of the words again; I just couldn't read it after he died. Although, I looked at it from time to time, to keep me connected. I hoped that it would have meaning for me again at some point.

Finally, five months to the day after Bob died, it did. It spoke to me as if Bob had written it personally to me. The word was "Honoring You":

### Honoring You (Sunday, September 7, 2008)

Thank you for being God's love in expression. My message of love to a special person in my life: I am in awe of the ways you have been there for me in the past and are here for me now. I give thanks for how greatly your caring touch has blessed me.

Your love, support, and encouragement have filled my life with assurance and inspiration. You have nourished me physically, mentally, and spiritually and therein have prepared me for an even brighter future.

Every day I bless you with loving thoughts and affirmative prayers. It is my great honor to give back to you in ways that you have shown joy and meaning to life. May you always be aware that God's loving presence is guiding and comforting you. Be assured, you are precious to me and have my everlasting love and support.

Reprinted with permission of Unity School of Christianity,

publisher of *The Daily Word*

**Action B:** Write down any positive thoughts you feel during the course of your day and look at them before you go to bed, or read something positive. Remember that your loved one who passed on wants you to be happy. If you separated from a relationship or have lost a body part, it can give you something else to focus on and help you realize there's more to your life than this loss.

**Action C:** Essential oils of bergamot, orange, grapefruit, coriander, and cilantro can help with positivity.

## 3. Ask Your Angels or Guides for Help

It's much easier to get through difficult times when we have support. Also, feeling alone leads to depression and despair. After Bob died, I was around people for a good length of time, and I also had my cat Fluffy to comfort me, so I was never lonely. However, there were many times when I still felt alone in the midst of all those people; I had lost that one person who would have my back, no matter what.

For example, I could tell Bob anything without being judged. Like the time when the toilet wouldn't flush in his parents' bathroom after I used it for a number two job, and I needed him to come take care of it for me. It would've been so much more embarrassing it I had to tell his parents instead.

While there are people you can turn to for help, they can't always be there, twenty-four hours a day; they have lives of their own they need to get back to. You can call on the universe, God, angels, guides, or whatever you believe in, any time of the day or night, to give you strength and support; this will keep you on your path to acceptance.

I believe we receive guidance and support all the time from the universe, but we need to dial in, just like finding a radio station, to hear it. By learning to trust our intuition and gut feelings, we can become more tuned into the answers and help we seek. As we ask, so shall we receive; the answers can come in many forms. For example, it could be an idea that suddenly pops into our heads, someone saying what we need to hear, or seeing the answer on a billboard.

Essential oils have long been used for connecting with angels. The energetic properties of each plant from which the oils are derived connect them to the earth, making them an effective way to create space for angelic or intuitive guidance. Choose an oil based on what you are asking help with. For example, to release anger, choose an oil for forgiveness.

It's actually a strength and not a weakness to ask for help and support. One of the things that gave me strength and inspiration is *Footprints in the Sand*, a poem written by Mary Stevenson in 1936. I love the notion that we are carried and supported through challenging times and that we don't have to go through them alone. During a meditation years ago, an image popped into my head that I was being rocked in God's arms. I guess this was my "footprints in the sand" moment of being supported on my journey. I always like to remember this image when I am experiencing difficult moments in my life.

---

**Action D:** Get in the habit of asking for help from wherever is comfortable for you. You can ask out loud or silently, or write it down. Remember that you are not alone in your experience.

---

## 4. Forgiveness

When we harbor anger, resentment, or hurt and continue to blame things on others or ourselves, we end up just hurting ourselves, emotionally and spiritually. So when we forgive, we're really releasing ourselves from these negative emotions that are causing stress in our bodies and minds. We need to stop beating ourselves (and others) up for things we have no control over in the first place in order to move on in the grief process and not get stuck, especially in the anger phase.

By forgiving, we actually honor the people we lost, for they want us to live the rest of our lives in happiness and joy, not bitterness or resentment. We allow ourselves to be released from the pains and hurts from the past, so we can move forward in our new normal lives and open us up to new possibilities.

To forgive, we only need to let go and release the emotions. It can be done as easily as with a deep breath or saying, "I forgive you" (the person doesn't have to be present). In fact, I was angry at Bob and God, who obviously weren't present, so I just said it out loud to them from inside my bedroom.

---

**Action E:** Write down a list of who you are angry with and cross them off as you find a way to forgive them. Remember that this exercise is more about helping yourself be free of the negativity of hurt and anger. By releasing these emotions, you are setting yourself free and unweighing your heart (kind of like what Scrooge was able to do at the end of *A Christmas Carol* by Charles Dickens).

---

**Action F:** Essential oils that help with forgiveness are bergamot and juniper berry. There is also a wonderful blend for forgiveness and letting go: two drops frankincense, one drop ylang-ylang, one drop lemongrass, one drop spikenard, and three drops white fir.

---

## 5. Gratitude

Like with positive thoughts, there's always something we can be grateful for, even when we're feeling the most down we've ever felt. When we're in a state of gratitude, it connects us to our higher spirit, inner peace, and joy. It keeps us focused on what we have rather than on what we're lacking, even if it's only one thing for a brief moment. That thread keeps us from falling into the pit of despair and puts us on the road to healing and acceptance.

---

**Action G:** Write down at least five things you're grateful for. You can add to it over time. Every morning and evening before going to bed, or anytime of the day that you need a boost, look at them and read them aloud by saying, "I am grateful for [insert whatever it is]."

---

**Action H:** Essential oils that help with gratitude are grapefruit, lime, bergamot, wild orange, ginger, and geranium.

---

## 6. The Art of Giving and Receiving

We need help to heal from grief, but when we help others, it can also help us by giving us a purpose, to contribute to others who are in need and maybe less fortunate than ourselves. No matter what we are going through, there are others who are suffering worse, and that can help us put things in perspective. It gives us a purpose in life, something beyond ourselves to live for.

Giving of our time by listening to someone, keeping them company, and giving them support are all ways we can practice the art of giving. We need to remember to allow others to give and contribute to us, as well. That keeps the giving and receiving cycle ongoing.

After Bob died and people would call me, it helped me if I asked about how they were doing. It helped me shift the focus of the tragedy I was going through and get away from everything being about me and what I was feeling.

---

**Action I:** Write down ways you can give, and do one of them at least once a week. Also, remember to do something nice for yourself at least once a week, as well. One of the nicest things I did for myself was to put a Jacuzzi tub in my bathroom so I could take a relaxing bath every week. It helped me unwind from the exhaustion of all the emotions I was feeling and the crying I was doing.

---

## 7. Love and Connection

The more we feel connected to God or people, animals, and nature, the more at peace and less anxious we feel. This is especially important during the holidays or birthdays or anniversaries. For me, the major holidays, like Christmas, weren't as difficult because we were always surrounded by other family members. Being alone on other special days, like birthdays and anniversaries, were more difficult for me, particularly after Bob passed because his birthday was the day before Valentine's Day. To help me cope those first several years, I went to visit my best friend from high school, who lives up in New England. Getting away helped me shift my attention from his birthday and Valentine's and gave me something completely different to do, including being in a different environment.

Sadness is an unfortunate part of life that we all feel at some point or another, but suffering is optional. We ultimately have a choice how we feel; we have the power to not stay victims to our circumstances and find a way to be the hero or heroine of our lives. What we live through not only can make us stronger and wiser, but as Bob used to say, "It gives us better stories to tell." We all have our journey in life; it is how we deal with the tragedies we endure that makes the difference in the quality of our lives moving forward. As we are able to open up our hearts again, like the Grinch, the more love we can feel for ourselves and others. Simultaneously, our fears and judgment dissipate. That is where true peace and acceptance lies.

---

**Action J:** When you feel isolated, instead of feeling sorry for yourself, try asking, "What can I do to feel more connected to people?" or "How can I open my heart to love again?" See what answers and ideas come up.

---

**Action K:** Cedarwood essential oil helps support connection and is very grounding and soothing, as well.

---

## Summary Review and Questions

1. Look up ways to meditate, and do at least five to ten minutes daily (preferably twenty to thirty minutes).

2. Write down your positive thoughts or read something positive.

3. Ask for help, whether it's from people or something bigger than yourself, like the universe or God.

4. Who do you need to forgive? Write their names down and cross them off as you forgive them.

5. What are you grateful for? Write them down and read them every morning and before going to bed.

6. Who or what organization can you give your time and attention to as a way to contribute?

7. What ways can you stay connected to the people or animals in your life when you feel isolated?

## Resource Guide

unity.com

dailyword.com

headspace.com

mayoclinic.org/healthy-living/adult-health/indepth/
forgvieness/art-20047692

abundance-and-happiness.com/gratitude.hmtl

artofgiving.in.net/

en.wikipedia.org/wiki/Meditation

healyourlife.com/daily-affirmations

ArlenePetrowsky.com

*From Grief to Joy: A Journey Back to Life and Living,* by
Donna Miesbach

# Notes and Journaling Pages

*If I should die and leave you here a while, be not like others sore undone, who keep long vigil by the silent dust. For my sake turn again to life and smile, nerving thy heart and trembling hand to do something to comfort other hearts than mine. Complete these dear unfinished tasks of mine and I perchance may therein comfort you.*

—Mary Hall, 1843–1927

## Conclusion

No matter how much we are put to the test in life, we can always find a way to rise above our circumstances, if we find the right pieces to put together a new normal life for ourselves. Life is meant for us to have challenges so we can learn, grow, and become stronger, if we allow it. That's why the hero's journey is one of the most popular stories in every indigenous culture. Joseph Campbell wrote about how the hero's journey spans through all cultures in his book *Hero of a Thousand Faces.*

Contrary to what we've been told, being a hero is not just for an elite few. We each can be the hero in the story of our lives and not remain a victim to our circumstances. To do so, all we need to do is claim our power of choice in how we deal with the things that happen to us. That is what makes the difference in the quality of our lives.

We all have two voices in our heads: the positive optimist who sees the glass as half-full (commonly depicted as the angel on our shoulder), and the negative pessimist who sees the glass as half-empty (commonly depicted as the devil on our shoulder). Whichever has the greater influence over your life, beliefs, choices, and decisions will determine your state of physical health, mental and emotional happiness, and spiritual joy.

I shared the top seven body, mind/emotional, and spiritual strategies that helped me find my new normal life three different times (when I lost my health, my husband, and my fiancé). I didn't accomplish these feats overnight, but I never gave up believing that I could achieve a new quality of life, which is what kept me going, even when I doubted that I could go on or would ever feel healthy, happy, or joyous again. Use the ones that speak to you. I had a saying I repeated when I was going through my journey to find my way back to health from being so ill with Crohn's; as I looked for the pieces to my puzzle, I said, "Take the best and leave the rest." Not all our puzzle pieces will be the same, as different strategies work for different people.

I pray these strategies can help give you ideas of how to put your new normal life back together and find your way back to feeling heathy and joy again. We must heal with our minds and our hearts. Don't let a tragedy put out the burning embers of light in your life. Life may dull our rays of light at times, but ultimately, we are all meant to be bright shining rays of light and fulfill our unique purpose. If you are having difficulty finding your way, you may call upon me to help guide you along the way.

Blessings,

Barbara

### Barbara Steingas

Radiant Life Coach
Physical Therapist
Health and Healing Specialist
Award-Winning Author

barbara@barbarasteingas.com
www.barbarasteingas.com
908.391.4463

"Helping You Find Health, Happiness & Joy"

*Email or call me to schedule a complimentary thirty-minute coaching session.*

## Epilogue

$\mathcal{J}$ want to leave you with a poem that is often read at funerals. The author, Henry Scott-Holland (1847–1918), a priest at St. Paul's Cathedral of London, did not intend it as a poem; it was actually delivered as part of a sermon in 1910. The sermon, titled, "Death: The King of Terrors," was preached while the body of King Edward VII was lying in state at Westminster.

I found this poem to be helpful in my healing process. Pray it may be of some comfort to you on your journey to finding your new normal life.

## Death Is Nothing At All

### By Henry Scott-Holland

Death is nothing at all.

It does not count.

I have only slipped away into the next room.

Nothing has happened.

Everything remains exactly as it was.

I am I, and you are you,

and the old life that we lived so fondly
together is untouched, unchanged.

Whatever we were to each other, that we are still.

Call me by the old familiar name.

Speak of me in the easy way which you always used.

Put no difference into your tone.

Wear no forced air of solemnity or sorrow.


Laugh as we always laughed at the little
jokes that we enjoyed together.

Play, smile, think of me, pray for me.

Let my name be ever the household
word that it always was.

Let it be spoken without an effort, without
the ghost of a shadow upon it.


Life means all that it ever meant.

It is the same as it ever was.

There is absolute and unbroken continuity.

What is this death but a negligible accident?

Why should I be out of mind because I am out of sight?

I am but waiting for you, for an interval,

somewhere very near,

just round the corner.


All is well.

Nothing is hurt; nothing is lost.

One brief moment and all will be as it was before.

How we shall laugh at the trouble of
parting when we meet again!

Printed in the United States
By Bookmasters